BURNETT OR BRIDGETT

A TALE OF TWO EMPLOYEES

Dr. Tracey C. Jones
AUTHOR OF *SPARK:*
5 ESSENTIALS TO IGNITE THE GREATNESS WITHIN

Published by Tremendous Leadership
PO Box 267 • Boiling Springs, PA 17007
(800) 233 - 2665 • *www.TremendousLeadership.com*

Burnett or Bridgett: A Tale of Two Employees.
Copyright © 2021 by Dr. Tracey C. Jones and Tremendous Leadership. All rights reserved. No part of this book may be reproduced or transmitted in any form or by any means, electronic or mechanical, including photocopying, recording, or by any information storage and retrieval system, without permission in writing from the publisher, except by a reviewer, who may quote brief passages in review.

Tremendous Leadership's titles may be bulk purchased for business or promotional use or for special sales. Please contact Tremendous Leadership for more information.

Tremendous Leadership and its logo are trademarks of Tremendous Leadership. All rights reserved.

A Tremendous EDGE and its logo are trademarks of Tremendous Leadership. All rights reserved.

ISBN-13 978-1-949033-54-0

Designed and Made in the United States of America

CONTENTS

Before We Begin..i
Leadership Versus Followership v
SOB and OCB: The Construct
   of Two Behaviors viii

PART I: BURNETT ~OR~ BRIDGETT
A TALE OF TWO EMPLOYEES   1

Paid to be Disengaged...2
The Stench of Stinkin' Thinkin' 5
It's Not Me 8
The RIGID Employee 11
From Fire Ball to Wrecking Ball......................14
Green Grass Syndrome 16
Working Together 19

PART II: BURN IT ~OR~ BRIDGE IT
THE LESSONS OF TWO EMPLOYEES   22

It Pays to Stay Engaged....................................23
Aromatic Actions 24
...It's YOU 25
Semper Gumby 26
Don't Burn the Ships 27
Separate the Wheat from the Chaff................31
Dodging Burnetts 33
It's Not Cool to Be a Fool................................35

THE EXPERT: DR. TRACEY C. JONES   37

Author, Speaker, Greatness Ignitor 37
Books...39
Keynotes..40
Corporate Workshops 40
Mergers & Acquisitions....................................40
Executive Mentoring...41

BEFORE WE BEGIN . . .

Growing up, I faithfully waited for the monthly *Highlights for Children* magazine. Inside of this treasure, a particular section fascinated me—a comic strip that contrasted the actions of two young, male, eponymous characters, Goofus and Gallant®. These illustrations, created by child psychologist and popular syndicated parental advice columnist, Garry Cleveland Myers, were so impactful I can still see them vividly in my mind. For those who haven't seen these personas in print, Gallant's actions represented responses and motives that were kind, right, and selfless, while Goofus's actions were mean, wrong, and selfish.

Since truth is timeless and human nature is what it is, I began to see these distinct personality profiles and performance patterns lived out in my young adulthood and into my middle years. I still recognize these two characters in every aspect of my life today, including myself. These depictions are much like the main character groups in another of my favorite reads, *Who Moved My Cheese* by Spencer Johnson, MD. In Johnson's tale, Sniff and Scurry are, well, gallantly Gallant in their drive to locate a new source of food, while Hem and Haw reflect the dilly-dally doofus of Goofus.

The two imaginary characters in the story you are about to read — Burnett and Bridgett — represent the impulses found within each of us, regardless of our age, gender, race, faith, or nationality. Like contemporary versions of Goofus and Gallant®, Burnett and Bridgett can be found in every enterprise that has ever existed or ever will exist. Those reading this story will recognize themselves and anyone else they have had the pleasure or pain of working for or with. Those who have taken up the managerial mantle or leadership laurel will also recognize these tell-tale traits and basis behaviors experienced in their supervisory positions throughout the years.

Leadership 101 teaches us that when faced with an employee issue, the leader must first determine if it is a *skill* problem or a *will* problem. Addressing a *skill* problem entails supplying additional training, clarifying expectations, providing needed resources, and gauging the employee's level of self-confidence. Assuming all of the means are in place, addressing a *will* problem is a much different issue and is entirely up to the employee to resolve because it is a function of followership, not of leadership. In other words, it's a heart issue, not a head issue. And guess which type 99% of the problems in your organizations will be? That's right—*will* problems manifested through toxic behaviors, poor work performance, hostile attitudes, and even sabotage.

This book is for leaders of all walks of life who deal with a problematic individual who re-

Before We Begin . . .

fuses to yield. One of the most difficult things to rightly comprehend is that we are responsible *to* people and not *for* people. There are times when a leader has to let someone fail. **You're going to find out, if you haven't already, that some people are wise in their own eyes while others seek to increase in learning.** The characters in this story are based not only on my professional experiences in five different industries over the past 40 years but also on my self-reflection about how I allowed my negative attitude to become my biggest hindrance in climbing the ladder of success. That's right — there were plenty of times I failed as a leader and as a follower.

Leaders spend far too much time watering dead plants and dangling carrots in front of those who aren't hungry. It's time to recognize and call destructive business behaviors for what they are and release them from your organization ASAP. Failure to hold your employees to the organizational standards will result in failure to accomplish the mission. **The purpose of this book is to help leaders clarify who needs to be on their team and who needs to go.** The sooner you take action, the better. This modern-day parable is about how to identify those who are willing to be developed, as opposed to those who won't be led, and to predict what will happen next due to these two *wills*. I've watched this pattern play out for the past 40 years, and, trust me, these situations end the same way every time.

All collaborative interactions are rooted in the submission of the individual's will for the organization's greater good. My father, Charlie "Tremendous" Jones, always said, "You can lead a horse to water, but you can't make him drink. But you can put salt in his oats and make him thirsty." Likewise, leadership is about bringing salt and light into the organization. But what if those workhorses in your stable not only refuse to drink but insist on poisoning the proverbial well? Like me, I'm guessing many of you have an instinctual sense when someone on your team isn't "all in."

This contemporary classic is designed to give you the confidence and courage to do what you need to do because it's not going to get better; in fact, it's going to get progressively worse, not just for you, but for everyone in the organization or in a business relationship with you. And if you happen to be one of those who isn't "feeling" your leadership, do the honorable thing and leave on good terms — sooner rather than later. You don't have to like your boss, but it is entirely unacceptable to fight your boss.

LEADERSHIP VERSUS FOLLOWERSHIP

The job doesn't make you; you make the job.
Charlie "Tremendous" Jones

I have lived and breathed leadership since I was a child. My father spoke and wrote on the topic of leadership his entire life. I grew up hearing speeches such as *The Price of Leadership* and *Where Does Leadership Begin?* I spent evenings at the dinner table listening to great men and women talk about finding great people and accomplishing great things by igniting, inspiring, and influencing their best. The roles and goals of those engaging in leadership were imprinted onto me as a child. Yet my father, and those under whose tutelage I sat, also taught me that leadership is a two-way street, a dance if you will; you can't lead those who won't be led. Even as a child, that much I understood.

Despite learning this invaluable truth at an early age, I went through decades at the best schools and cutting-edge organizations, observing a pronounced lack of understanding about what leadership truly is and why it only exists in the form of individual motivation. General George S. Patton concluded that the most important truth of leading others is to know how a person reacts.

Of course, there is no shortage of the prototypic bad boss in movies, books, blogs, and real life, but what about the bad employee?

Why don't we call out a failure of followership as often as we harp on a failure of leadership? One of my favorite memes proclaims, "Stop trying to make 'not your people' your people." Shouldn't that hold in the professional realm as well?

> I prefer a loyal staff officer to a brilliant one.
> **Gen. George S. Patton**

Much of the leadership teaching out there misses the mark because it ignores the integrative, dyadic aspects of leadership. **The flip side of the leadership coin is followership.** For decades, I thought that I was a flawed and failed leader because I bought into the "prevailing" wisdom that if an employee is unmotivated, disengaged, or even disrespectful, *I* was wholly at fault. But then, I began to realize how pervasive this deceitfully damning directive mission drift had become. This relativistic, societal shift from integrative leadership was doing nothing more than encouraging employees to shirk their personal responsibilities for ownership, growth, and collective engagement. As my father also said, "You're never a failure until you blame somebody else." Imagine how this type of tough love and universal truth would play out in today's human resources, legal divisions, and training departments.

So, when I began my doctoral studies in the field of—you guessed it—leadership, I immedi-

Leadership Versus Followership

ately honed my research into the field of followership. Robert Kelley's book, *The Power of Followership*, was an epiphany for me as a lifelong student and lover of all things leadership. I integrated his construct of the different types of followers into almost every single presentation I gave and everything I wrote, including my children's books.

Two essential elements are necessary for a truly world-class organization: critical thinking skills and all-in engagement. Without those two essentials flowing freely between every single employee, regardless of rank or tenure, you're not going to get where you want to go, and as Shakespeare said, there'll be "something rotten in the state of Denmark." Many of you already smell an organizational stench in your place of work.

The most important task of any leader is picking the right people. **That's because success in any enterprise takes two to tango—leaders who lead and followers who follow.** Feedback is only heard by those who have the mission goals of the organization inside of them.

Burnett or Bridgett

SOB AND OCB: THE CONSTRUCT OF TWO BEHAVIORS

> The man who fails to give fair service during
> the hours for which he is paid is dishonest.
> The man who is not willing to give more
> than this is foolish.
> ***Charles Schwab***

In life, we must decide whether we will live our lives for ourselves or for something beyond ourselves. I call the first allegiance SOB, which stands for ***Self-Oriented Behaviors***. The latter allegiance reflects a leadership term called OCB, which stands for ***Organizational Citizenship Behaviors***. OCBs are covered extensively in my favorite leadership construct, Leader-Member Exchange, or LMX. You're either in with the leader, or you're out.

In this parable, Burnett is similar to Goofus. In case you haven't caught the play on words in the name, Burnett wants to burn down everyone and everything because she thinks she is the only one who knows anything and that everyone else is expendable or an annoyance. Bridgett is like Gallant. She always looks to bridge any experience, good, bad, or ugly, into something transformational. She embraces her integration into the entity.

Burnetts operate on their own wavelengths. **Although they initially appear to be supporting the needs and goals of the col-**

lective, it soon becomes evident that it is their way or the highway. Their pride morphs into hubris manifested by over-inflated perceptions of their capabilities. Their humility devolves into false humility displayed in their self-righteous and offended responses. While leaders focus on bringing out the best, Burnetts give the leader the beast. Leaders spend an excessive amount of their time, energy, and resources dealing with these emotional vampires. I once heard them described as CAVE people: Citizens Against Virtually Everything!

> Staff officers of inharmonious disposition, irrespective of their ability, must be removed.
> A staff cannot function properly unless it is a united family.
> ### Gen. George S. Patton

Bridgetts, on the other hand, operate on the frequency of the collective. They have an inner dialogue that goes like this: **What do I have to learn? How can I improve? Who Can Teach Me?** They desire to improve more than they desire to be correct, making them team members who can take risks, own mistakes, and not take offense. They know they have a great deal to offer and to learn. As Ralph Waldo Emerson said, "Every man I meet is my superior in some way, in that, I can learn from him." Because of this coding, they exhibit OCBs to an exemplary degree. They go above and beyond what is required of them, and they display the three Rs of humility with every team member: respect, regard, and recognition of interdependence.

Now, this is where our story begins....

PART I
BURNETT ~or~ BRIDGETT
A TALE OF TWO EMPLOYEES

Burnett and Bridgett are working for the same employer. They have both had various jobs before this one and are conscientious, intelligent, and diligent. From a performance perspective, they are both capable of high-quality work, self-regulating, and problem-solving. During the first six months on the job, both employees are perceived as fully engaged, executing projects that delight their boss, Frank. These two are regarded as exceptional performers marked for increased responsibilities, titles, and wages—or so leadership thinks. As in every relationship, however, when the honeymoon period is over, only then do we begin to see the true identity of the other person.

At the six-month point, a slight divergence between the two employees begins to manifest itself. Although the *capability* is still present in both Burnett and Bridgett, the *intentionality* has left one of them, if it was even there to begin with. Someone has gone off the grid and isn't coming back . . .

Burnett or Bridgett

PAID TO BE DISENGAGED

The soul of the sluggard craves and gets nothing, while the soul of the diligent is richly supplied.
Proverbs 13:4

Burnett and Bridgett are both involved in the new Customer Relationship Management (CRM) database roll-out the company has been planning for the past two years; hence, there is a lot at stake with plenty of moving pieces. Each of them has a crucial position and meets regularly with their working groups.

As Bridgett begins her day updating her metrics and schedule, she sees her co-worker on her computer deep in thought.

"What are you working on, Burnett?" asks Bridgett. The two share the same cubicle space and often dialogue about what they are doing.

"Work!" exclaims Burnett. "My work," she adds with a grin. "I've got this great side hustle. Just getting the project ready for my client."

"But you're on the clock," Bridgett responds uneasily.

"I know, but for as hard as I work, this company owes me. I should be making way more than they are paying me, so this is how I make it right."

"Burnett, isn't that unethical?"

"No, it's not," Burnett snaps. "They didn't tell me I couldn't do it, so it's better to ask for

Paid to be Disengaged

Burnett uses company time to work on her own projects leaving her co-workers to pick up the slack.

Bridgett respects her co-workers and dutifully puts in a full day's work.

forgiveness than permission! They probably wouldn't like it that I connected with some of these clients through work, anyway. Plus, with all the time and money wasted by management, they've already set a precedent. I've seen the bonuses they give themselves. So, I don't feel bad about using company time to work on my advanced degree, plan my vacation, or take extended lunches. It's just my way of getting what's owed to me."

"I've heard several of your team members complaining that you are falling behind and they have to pick up the slack. Now I understand why that's happening. What if they did this to you?"

"I've got it covered, Bridgett," Burnett retorts. "I've got Dave making sure the deliverables get completed and turned in. I work smarter, not harder, Bridgett. You should try it sometime."

Bridgett doesn't know what to say. She works really hard to be an excellent steward of company time and resources. In fact, if she has to take a personal call, she limits it to urgent matters only. She's pursuing higher education, too, but she plans her school requirements around her work schedule. But she has noticed that Burnett has been taking leave as soon as it accrues and has even started missing deadlines, and she tells Burnett that it's not cool.

THE STENCH OF STINKIN' THINKIN'

*A fool's lips walk into a fight,
and his mouth invites a beating.*
Proverbs 18:6

Later that week, Bridgett and Burnett decide to go out for drinks with their colleagues after work. Burnett claims a seat next to her cubicle mate and spends the entire time venting about their boss and the company.

"I can't wait for Fridays!" Burnett exclaims. "I can't stand working with those idiots. I mean, how they are even in business is a miracle. Most of those people there have no clue what we do and are worthless as leaders. I know way more than they do."

"Wow, Burnett, where did this horrible attitude come from?" Bridgett couldn't help but respond. "They're not all that bad. And we've got stable jobs with great benefits. Most people would kill for what we have."

"Of course, I have a horrible attitude," quips Burnett. "Who wouldn't? They are just so clueless. Anybody with half a brain can see it," she continued, completely ignoring Bridgett's perspective. "I sit in those meetings and can't believe these are the people running our organization."

"Have you brought any of this to the attention of management?" Bridgett prods. "I mean, are there specific things that they should be looking at?"

"Why should I? If they're too stupid to notice, that's their problem. They get paid the big bucks, so they should be able to figure it out. Frank asked me about a project I was working on just the other day, and I let him have it. I mean, just let me do my work, and I'll tell you what you need to know! They'd be in a huge mess if I weren't here keeping it all together. So, they just need to let me do my thing and go back to their offices."

"Do you talk to your family and friends this way, Burnett? I really don't think it's healthy."

"Yes, I do! And you know what's also not healthy, Bridgett? Being an idiot. That's on them, not me. I could go anywhere and make twice as much as I'm making. They're lucky to have me."

Once again, Bridgett is speechless. She may not always agree with every decision made, but she makes sure her demeanor and communication responses are always professional and calm. She knows that Burnett engages in water cooler gossip and happy hour cliques, creating an "us" versus "them" atmosphere in the organization that further alienates her, and those who come under her influence, from management. Bridgett does her best to steer clear of workplace drama, but she and the other team members are finding it harder and harder with all of Burnett's complaining.

The Stench of Stinkin' Thinkin'

Burnett has a critical spirit towards her boss and engages in disruptive drama in the workplace.

Bridgett keeps her communications professional and respectful at all times and with all people.

Burnett or Bridgett

IT'S NOT ME...

By insolence comes nothing but strife, but
with those who take advice is wisdom.
Proverbs 13:10

Burnett's boss, Frank, had assigned a deliverable last month. With the due date approaching, he picks up the phone to ask her about the status.

"Hi Burnett, this is Frank. Just wondering what's going on with the new marketing campaign piece I needed to be uploaded."

"That won't be ready for several more weeks," Burnett replies. "The IT folks are backed up with the CRM database roll-out, and nothing is getting through."

"Wait a minute, Burnett, I gave this to you last month. I even followed up, and you assured me that everything was fine. And *now*," he emphasizes the word in frustration, "you're telling me we're another couple weeks out?"

"Don't you dare come at me, Frank!" she yells.

"That is unacceptable, Burnett. I need an updated status on what you are going to do to draw back in this timeline." Frank hangs up the phone, utterly astounded.

How could she yell at me when all I was asking for was an update?

Reflecting on the previous six months, Frank wonders what may have happened to initiate or

It's Not Me . . .

Burnett is offended when given constructive feedback because she is driven by the need to be right.

Bridgett uses constructive feedback to learn and grow because she is driven by the desire to be developed.

exacerbate this situation and what he can do to bring Burnett back into the organizational fold. When he had asked her a few weeks ago if she needed assistance or any adjustments to the workload or requirements, she had given him virtually no input. Instead, she had answered him with a terse "no" as if she were offended that he had even asked. She quipped that she was fully engaged and had everything that she needed.

Several previous interactions come to his mind as he realizes that these subtle slips and snarks have been happening all along the way. As he thinks more about it, he recognizes that Burnett's communications with him have become increasingly rude and have a sarcastic edge to them. In fact, he realizes that he has begun dreading any interaction with his previously stellar employee and walking on eggshells around her.

Frank has come to the realization that this toxic attitude may have been there all along, hiding just beneath the surface.

THE RIGID EMPLOYEE

A scoffer does not like to be reproved;
he will not go to the wise.
Proverbs 15:12

During a team meeting later in the week, Burnett insists on arguing about a shift in

The RIGID Employee

priorities. Even though she is not the team lead, she heartily expresses her disagreement with the change in direction they are taking with the campaign. When the meeting is over, the team lead pulls Burnett aside.

"That was uncalled for in there, Burnett. You spoke out of turn and acted like you were the key decision-maker. I told you this change was not up for discussion."

As Burnett silently slinks back to her desk, Bridgett can see the steam coming out of her ears.

"What's wrong, Burnett?"

"Nothing," snaps Burnett. But then she proceeds to complain, "The team leader has a lot of gall questioning my input and scheduling. They need to leave me alone to do what only I know how to do."

"Well, they still have to check in and get updates on what you're working on…. what all of us are working on."

"Not me, they don't. And they're going to be sorry they did!" Burnett is clearly angered by Bridgett's response, apparently assuming her co-worker would be on her side. "If they don't want me to express my opinion at meetings, then I'm not going to say anything, not a word. And you can bet they won't be getting any of my support, that's for sure."

For the third time in as many weeks, Bridgett is stunned. Not only is she thankful for her job, but she is also fulfilled. Even when she disagrees with management, she would never dream of pushing back on directives and badmouthing them the way Burnett does. If she has an issue with her boss or co-workers, she takes it to them directly for resolution in a professional manner.

Although Burnett doesn't realize it, or doesn't care, her boss is made aware of what happened during and after the team meeting. He meets with HR who share that they have also received reports that she often gets emotional or engages in argumentative behavior in retaliation when someone goes against her ideas. He is reminded of the leadership seminar he attended recently where the speaker introduced an acronym for people who are RIGID: **R**efusing **I**nput **G**iven to **I**nfluence **D**evelopment.

Frank has also received reports from Burnett's team members of having to cover for her. He is even hearing rumors that she has delegated many of her assignments to a "helper" who actually produces the work that she turns in. One co-worker says he has tried to address the issues affecting the team deliverables with Burnett directly, but she blows the problems out of proportion, causing the rest of the team to have to work around her rather than with her. Burnett has told Frank she is fully engaged, but her actions seem to tell a different story.

The RIGID Employee

Burnett is inflexible when it comes to shifting organizational priorities and lets everyone know it.

Bridgett understands the changing nature of business and works with her boss to adapt to any new challenges and tasks.

Burnett or Bridgett

From Fire Ball to Wrecking Ball

Pride goes before destruction, and a haughty spirit before a fall.
Proverbs 16:18

"I can't believe they are doing this!" exclaims Burnett, upset the new customer feedback results are in, and the company needs to pivot accordingly. "Here they are again changing focus midstream. It's a wonder they are still in business. I wish they would make up their minds about what in the heck we're supposed to focus on."

"I don't think it's that big of a deal," Bridgett tries to soothe her, even though she doesn't understand why Burnett is taking the new strategy change so personally. "It's their company, and we are still getting paid. So, nothing has changed for us in terms of completing the work they assign us to do."

"They start one thing and then change to another. It shows they don't have a clue what they are doing."

"It's just business—and it's *their* business, Burnett. That's what being an owner is. They have to absorb all the risk; therefore, they get to make all the calls. They aren't asking us to do anything illegal, immoral, or unethical. And these are changes all of us are being asked to comply with, not just you."

Burnett waves off her friend, shaking her

head and stewing at her computer.

When Frank stops by a little later to setup a time to review these performance issues, Burnett insists on arguing with him about the new direction and tasks assigned. "Well, Frank, I'll do it, but I'm not happy about it," she rolls her eyes, her new favorite method of feedback, putting her superiority on full display. "This new work is a complete waste of my time."

Frank now sees the pattern clearly and knows Burnett will not do what is requested of her without fighting all the time. Frank knows that Burnett's hypersensitivity will twist anything he says into a personal offense. He is savvy enough to know that if someone is incapable of accepting feedback, they cannot function as a member of the team. He knows in his heart that Burnett will never be a part of the team and has wholly checked out.

With all doors of open and authentic communication from Burnett closed, Frank begins preparing for the inevitable by gradually pulling responsibilities off of Burnett and placing them elsewhere.

Burnett or Bridgett

GREEN GRASS SYNDROME

A heart at peace gives life to the body, but
envy makes the bones rot.
Proverbs 14:30

"I've had it! I can't take any more of this! I am so done with this place!" Burnett exclaims one afternoon.

"What happened?" Bridgett asks, slightly startled.

"They think I don't do anything here. I'll show them," Burnett retorts. She seems to be fueled by a sense of self-righteousness as she bangs away on her keyboard, proud to be "putting others in their place."

Bridgett sits in shock. Although she knows Burnett hasn't been happy, she can't believe her friend is throwing what is tantamount to a temper tantrum.

"I already interviewed for another job, and I'm taking it…. NOW."

Bridgett can't help but wonder if Burnett's new employer will ask why their new hire can show up for work the very next day. She watches as Burnett hastily fires off an email copying everyone in the organization about her immediate exit and how much of a loser she thinks her boss is. Throwing her keys and badge on the desk, she grabs a few personal items and walks off without another word.

Frank comes looking for Burnett as soon as

Green Grass Syndrome

Burnett departs the organization with the intention of causing as much distress as possible.

Bridget departs giving plenty of notice so her boss and team members are positioned to continue moving forward.

he gets the email, but she has already left the building. He and Bridgett look at each other in disbelief and shrug their shoulders. "I'm sorry to put you in this position, Bridgett. We're going to have to work extra hard to make sure things don't get dropped."

"Don't worry, Frank; it's not your fault. I'm sure we'll figure it out."

"I think Burnett is suffering from the Green Grass Syndrome," Frank shakes his head.

"Green Grass Syndrome?" Bridgett looks puzzled. "What's that?"

"You've heard the saying, 'The grass is always greener on the other side of the fence.' Well, Green Grass Syndrome is the common misperception that the next job, boss, co-worker, house, partner—the next whatever—will be precisely what you are looking for and deserve," Frank explains solemnly. "Unfortunately, I'm afraid this cycle will continue until Burnett owns her need to grow and improve."

"Well, she certainly was miserable," Bridgette agrees. "Her departure is actually a blessing. Now we can focus on getting the work done and not arguing about it."

And with that, they both breathe a sigh of relief.

Frank has realized the true nature of the person he and his employees have been dealing with over the past year, and her abrupt departure confirms that. Of course, Burnett's co-workers are extremely angry about her sudden decision, frustrated that they were not even worth one day of transition from Burnett. And since Burnett wasn't prone to sharing anything, they'll have to figure out what has gotten left where and begin to pick up the pieces. They are all looking forward to the day someone will ask their opinion of her. As can be expected, Burnett blocks all of her former co-workers on social media. It is as if she never worked there at all, and it is certain that she won't be getting any help in the future in the way of references or recommendations.

WORKING TOGETHER

Before you go running off to what you think are greener pastures, make sure that your own is not just as green or perhaps even greener. It has been said that if the other guy's pasture appears to be greener than ours, it is quite possible that it is getting better care. Besides, while you are looking at other pastures, other people are looking at yours.

Earl Nightingale

Unlike her former co-worker, Bridgett strives to be an integral part of her team and goes beyond the minimum threshold of expectations. She keeps Frank informed of any situation requiring his time or attention, and in return, Frank makes adjustments for Bridgett's

Burnett or Bridgett

requests as needed. She provides feedback on issues and fully backs decisions once made.

Although Bridgett knows this is not her dream job, she sees the bigger picture regarding her professional development and does her best during her tenure at the organization. She is gaining the most valuable employee collateral in the world—experience. She values this fact, knowing it will open the next door in her career path. Bridgett also knows that the more she puts into the job, the more she gets out of it.

When the time comes for her to tender her resignation, Bridgett asks to speak to her boss personally.

"Sure, Bridgett, what's up?" Franks responds easily.

"Well, you know I have been dealing with taking care of my mother," Bridgett begins. "And it looks like I need to pick a job closer to her home and with a bit more flexibility in my hours."

"I knew you were dealing with this, Bridgett, and I really appreciate you keeping us in the loop. I just have to ask, is there anything at all we can do to make this work and keep you on board?" Frank's voice exudes compassion and sincerity.

"Thanks so much for saying that, Frank!" Bridgett smiles, feeling valued. "I'll never forget what we did here as a team, but I need to move on to the next chapter."

Working Together

"I know you'll leave us with everything we need, Bridgett, but we sure will miss you. Let me know what I can do for your new job; a letter of recommendation, COBRA, you name it."

"I sure will take you up on that recommendation, and I would like to enroll in the COBRA benefits until I can get picked up with my new job. It's been an honor working here, Frank, and I'm going to miss you, too. Thanks for everything you taught me!"

Once Bridgett gives proper notice for her resignation, she continues to work at her job as if she isn't leaving. In fact, she actually works harder. She wants to finish strong and ensure she leaves all of the projects she has been working on in exceptional shape.

Bridgett's farewell party is a testament to the kindness and conscientiousness she shows to everyone she interacts with. When she shares her news via social media, she has nothing but wonderful words for her co-workers and company. To this day, Frank still keeps in touch with her to see how her mother is doing and to let her know she is welcome back at any time.

PART II
BURN IT ~or~ BRIDGE IT
THE LESSONS OF TWO EMPLOYEES

The best preparation for tomorrow's work is
to do your work as well as you can today.
Elbert Hubbard

Early in the story, we see that Frank is perplexed over what is happening as he watches his once model employee insist on bending the company to meet her demands rather than aligning with the organization's needs. The seemingly once all-in Burnett starts to express critical words to her co-workers and even her boss. She begins sharing her sense of offense with other team members, including Bridgett. Bridgett asks Burnett where this change in attitude came from but gets no information. The once bright shining star has turned into an energy-sucking black hole. But her boss doesn't understand yet that Burnett has a very different nature than the one publicly portrayed during the first six months. As stated earlier, leadership is a heart-revealing exercise and what's inside a person eventually comes out.

It Pays to Stay Engaged

In every relationship, when the honeymoon period is over, only then do we begin to see the true identity of the other person. So it is only after Burnett's mask comes off can leadership see what's underneath.

IT PAYS TO STAY ENGAGED

If you want a better boss, be a better employee.
Dr. Tracey C. Jones

As the story progresses, we see that the more Burnett self-isolates and performs in her silo, thanks to her prickly demeanor, the more superior she feels to everyone else in the organization, including her boss. Because of her perceived superiority, Burnett has no qualms about engaging in a side hustle or working on her advanced degree while she's still on the clock. She feels she is owed so much more in compensation for her exceptional skills, so this is just her way of collecting what is actually due to her.

Burnetts are driven by self-gratification rather than self-offering. Their motivations are for personal glory rather than professional gain. Their self-oriented behaviors make them incapable of being integrated parts of the collective. When employees secure their boats to your organizational island, the goal is for them to draw nearer to your shores, to disembark, and to take up residence. But when you hire Burnetts, you'll begin noticing that they insist on trying to pull the organization out to their boats, an impossible, unethical, and idiotic activity. Burnetts insist they know best and to hell with the rest.

On the other hand, we see that Bridgett is committed to exchanging an honest day's work for her pay. She feels a sense of obligation to her team and is compelled to do right by them. She is thankful for the opportunity to draw a salary, and her actions reflect this sense of gratitude. Rather than feeling like she is unfairly compensated, Bridgett feels the drive to make the organization better each day.

Aromatic Actions

Behave so that the aroma of your actions may enhance the general sweetness of the atmosphere.
Henry David Thoreau

At the root of Burnett's refusal to articulate any resources she requires is an inflated sense of importance and a deep need for excessive attention and admiration. Burnetts want to make sure that they are seen as saviors without whom the organization could not exist. Leader beware; unless you are unwavering in your adoration of Burnetts, they'll quickly turn on you because underneath their competent exteriors lie pronounced disdain for authority figures.

Authentic leaders tend to their employees like shepherds over their flocks. If something is amiss, they address it and seek ways to link individual motivations to missional ones. However, Burnetts refuse to disclose the roots of their unhappiness, making it impossible for their bosses to ascertain a cause and devise a solution. This silent treatment is because Burnetts are not interested in answers; they are interested only in self-serving suffering, which poisons the entity. They take everything, even innocuous comments, as insults and are offended by everything and everyone. Leaders cannot figure out the root cause, as Burnetts cannot own their part in the solution. Anything not dealt with regarding a shared unity to the mission will continue to metastasize until cut out.

...It's YOU

Men who do things without being told draw the most wages.
Rodney Dangerfield

Burnett's need to be right extinguishes her need to improve. Thus, any corrective interaction only serves to escalate Burnett's sarcasm toward her boss or team members. In her mind, if she is questioned, that means she is no longer in control. When Burnetts get rebuked, expect blow-back. They have an overwhelming need to appear blameless.

When team members refuse accountability, there is no longer a team. Hence, this type of behavior is sabotaging. They may still be "on" the job, but they have checked out. They may be working against you and most likely are. If you cannot freely give input with a reasonable expectation that it will be heard and acted upon, that person is incapable of being a good follower. And leaders can't lead people who refuse to follow.

SEMPER GUMBY

There can be no life without change, and to be afraid of what is different or unfamiliar is to be afraid of life.
Theodore Roosevelt

Today's organizations must adapt at the speed of light. Transparency, interconnected marketplaces, increasing regulatory requirements, and global communications all mean that, on any given day, for-profit and non-profit entities must constantly evaluate previously made decisions for any tactical tweaks and strategic shifts. As a result, what may have seemed like a sound decision last quarter, could need some serious finessing in the current one as leaders balance resources, opportunities, threats, shareholders, public opinion, and the bottom line.

In the story, Burnett becomes angrier and more entrenched with every staff meeting. She thinks any adaptation to what she was initially told to do is wrong and lets everyone at the table know so. She regards leadership as clueless and disorganized. She sees every management decision as dichotomous, not realizing that these adaptations are for the organization's overall health—including hers. Burnett is rigid, and that causes her to make emotional decisions, throwing the proverbial baby out with the bathwater.

Rigid thinking and reactive behaviors make it hard for individuals to adapt to changing situations, causing disruption to their personal, professional, and social lives. In psychology, *rigidity*, or *mental rigidity*, refers to an obstinate inability to yield or a refusal to appreciate another person's viewpoint or emotions characterized by a lack of empathy. Remember the acronym for **RIGID: Refusing Input Given to Influence Development**.

To combat this kind of rigid thinking, the Marine Corps has an unofficial motto: *Semper Gumby*. With this play on their official motto, "*Semper Fidelis*," which means "Always Faithful," they translate "*Semper Gumby*" to mean "Always Flexible." It's a motto that we should probably all adopt.

Don't Burn the Ships

If you work for a man, for God's sake, work for him. If he pays you your bread and butter, think well of him, speak well of him.
Elbert Hubbard

Burnett or Bridgett

Because Burnett is all about herself, she lacks the respectful, professional, and adult manners to end a working relationship. So offended is she by what she perceives as management's gross ineptitude and inability to see her greatness, she doesn't even bother with offering her two weeks' notice. Instead, her departure is reckless, emotional, and reactionary, all behaviors not acceptable in any professional culture with shared roles and responsibilities. But Burnett never owns the fact that she was part of a collective. Two weeks, let alone two days, or even two minutes, is far too long for her to suffer fools anymore.

When employees walk off jobs, they might as well have never worked there at all. They can't use their previous employers for references. They probably shouldn't even use them as experience on their resume because they wouldn't want anyone to contact them.

Healthy employer-employee relationships end all the time. In a healthy decoupling, both parties acknowledge it is time to move on. They each own their parts in what they accomplished and, if under less than desirable circumstances, what they could have done better or what they will do better in the future.

But Burnetts are incapable of seeing any wrongdoing in themselves, choosing instead to fixate on the issues with everyone else. Prone to assigning accusations, Burnetts must find fault

Don't Burn the Ships

when professional relationships end. Hence, these followers will never evolve and grow because they are too busy placing blame. This cycle will repeat, as do all character malformations and wounds, until the individual addresses the root of their responses. Most likely, the root is pride. Don't be surprised if/when your Burnett cuts all ties, blocks any previous connections, and lawyers up. They do not tend to go off quietly into the sunset without biting back in some way, shape, or form. They need to punish you and the organization.

Because Burnetts are incapable of examining their motives in light of a larger, missional construct, the motivation at work has always been about them; you just missed it. But don't beat yourself up; it happens. Don't mourn—move on. Do some serious self-reflection to understand why you as a leader allowed this type of dysfunctional behavior to stay in the organization for as long as you did and how you missed it in the first place.

Then, please do what you need to do to ensure it doesn't happen again. Of course, you'll never know exactly who you are on-boarding until they embark on the ship and you set sail. However, you can move decisively when you see these tell-tale signs that they will not become a part of the crew, head back to a safe harbor, and let them disembark.

The mark of being grateful is to bring things

to an orderly end. And that is exactly what Bridgett did. She had kept her boss and team members aware of an ill parent and gave them plenty of time to begin shifting work requirements so that the productivity continues seamlessly.

> Great is the art of beginning,
> but greater is the art of ending.
> **_Henry Wadsworth Longfellow_**

The Bureau of Labor Statistics (BLS) published a study from 2019 that looked at the number of jobs held between the ages of 18 and 60. It turns out that the average person has 12 jobs! I have worked in five different industries across the globe during the span of my professional experience. And I show no signs of slowing down. My average tenure was approximately three years until I landed in my true calling. My father always told me, "You can work for someone else, or you can work for yourself. Until you work for yourself, you'll always hit the wall." I also learned service before self in the military. So as much as I was sure I wasn't going to make any of those jobs my long-term vocational calling, I sure went all-in until my last minute on the payroll. And I never put out any negative or derogatory feedback regarding my previous employers.

We all can learn an essential life lesson from the parable of the tortoise and the hare. Employees are remembered for how they exit an organization, not how they started. Anyone who has been through a breakup of any sort is well aware of this fact. **Don't burn the ships; this is work, not war.** You never want to slam the door so hard it ends up smacking you in the face. Always leave on better terms than when you started. And always depart in such a manner that if the opportunity should ever arise for your employer to hire you back on in any capacity—stranger things have happened—they'd be thrilled to do so. And your co-workers would be happy too.

SEPARATE THE WHEAT FROM THE CHAFF

Yet do not miss the moral, my good men....
Take the wheat and let the chaff lie still.
Geoffrey Chaucer

This EDGE was born out of a moment when I realized I had once again allowed a Burnett into my organization. After lamenting that I had disregarded my intuition and refused to confront the warning signals and bad behavior, I wondered why on earth I even bothered to get a PhD in Leadership.

And then one of my friends said to me, "That's happened to me so many times, too!" And another chimed in as well, and another, and another. It seemed that I wasn't the only employer who had experienced this—repeatedly.

An overwhelming percentage of the calls and messages I get are from leaders looking for counsel on how to handle a Burnett. Twenty years ago, someone gave me a magnet for my refrigerator that read, "It's not the people you fire that make your life miserable; it's the ones you don't." Truer words were never spoken.

Nothing will kill a great employee faster than watching leadership tolerate a bad one. In other words, if employees aren't fired with enthusiasm, they should be! If not, you, my dear fellow leader, will suffer the consequences, as will your organization. Leaders know the workplace is a collective gathering for the greater good of the organization. That's why they have mission statements. Anything that detracts from that mission needs to be cut loose. As I stated earlier, they don't have to like you, but they sure as heck can't fight you.

Leaders need to remember that there's no such thing as genius — only application and self-discipline. Therefore, when you feel like you have an employee on the payroll who has you between a rock and a hard place, let them go. The world will not end. No human being is indispensable. You can't get it right without the right people, and Burnetts are wrong on so many levels.

So, stop trying to get the Burnetts on your team to fit into the "right" hole. They won't, not ever, not in a million years. Seriously; let it go. There are other fish in the organizational ocean, fish that would love to swim in your missional seas! Go find your Bridgetts!

Dodging Burnetts

The past sharpens perspective, warns against pitfalls, and helps to point the way.
Dwight D. Eisenhower

So, what's a leader to do? You must be thinking, "If you missed it, Tracey, what about me?" Looking back on my history with Burnetts, here is my advice. As I mentioned earlier, while employees may appear confident and capable in the initial stages, you never really know someone until after the honeymoon period is over. Burnetts interview well. They are typically charismatic and assertive. They may even bring up ideas about your business. At first, you may be tempted to think, "This person is too good to be true!" Well, hold that thought.

There are several tells that tend to tip off a wise leader. First, Burnetts will be highly critical of their current or last organization. They will tell you how hard they have worked to influence the culture for the best, but the leadership is so lame that they can do nothing else. They'll convince you they need to soar with the eagles, not troll with the turkeys, and that's your first hint. All of us have left bad jobs and bad bosses. However, we never bad-mouth a previous employer as a person. We can share how some deliverables or values did not feel congruent with us, but we never run down a last boss or co-worker. If your prospective Burnett does this, it'll only be a matter of time (six months by my research) before you become the object of their scorn.

The only way to avoid a wrong hiring decision is to do your due diligence. You wouldn't get married on your first date, so take your time and conduct a professional courtship. Call up that boss they so desperately despise and get, as Paul Harvey said, "the rest of the story." Be sure to vet your candidates with multiple previous employers, not just with the references they supplied. As they say, "Slow to hire, quick to fire."

Second, you may hear side comments or quips about the salary, time off, benefits, location of the office, desk size, you name it. Now I am all for negotiating the best deal, but Burnetts do it in a way that lets you know they'll be telling you what's acceptable and not the other way around. This sniping is because they are quick to pull these subtle power plays and you, because you assume they are such superstars, are all too willing to comply.

Third, the best way to avoid this is to build in a probationary period and ensure you get a plethora of feedback from numerous levels and areas. Burnetts often show different sides to different groups of people. Once this probationary period is completed, then you can validate any perks commensurate with performance. Do not promise them the moon before they are even on your payroll. You'll live to regret it, I promise.

Lastly, watch for one of two types of classic Burnett communication styles: sarcastic quips letting you know that they are smarter than you (bragging), and cones of silence whereby they leave you in the dark because you don't need to know (stonewalling).

If you do these three things, you can dodge those bullets named Burnett!

IT'S NOT COOL TO BE A FOOL

*The way of fools seems right to them,
but the wise listen to advice.*
Proverbs 12:15

Several years ago, I read the book of Proverbs from start to finish as a requirement for one of my doctoral leadership classes. I was blown away! How had I missed all this grounded wisdom? If I had only been more diligent in studying this book during my development as a leader, it would have made an enormous difference not only for me but also for those in my organization.

Proverbs is the most remarkable leadership book of all time. King Solomon's sound wisdom has been read, studied, revered, and tested throughout the millennia by people of all worldviews and walks. As a result, it "overfloweth" with pragmatic, applicable, and timeless truths about how we are—and are not—to interact with employers, employees, spouses, lenders, judges, children, parents, friends, neighbors, elected leaders, and even animals! You have read a sampling of these truths scattered throughout this book. Interestingly enough, the word *fool* appears 40 times in the ESV version of Proverbs. The ways of the fool are contrasted with the ways of the wise, just like with Burnett and Bridgett.

There are 31 chapters in Proverbs, and I would highly encourage each of you to begin your day reading one chapter. That means you'll get through the book of Proverbs 12 times in a single year! And, most importantly, you stay focused on the root cause of the issue at hand and not confused by all the other relativistic "prevailing" wisdom.

Thus ends our modern-day parable found in organizations across the globe. Now go forth confidently and the next time you walk into your place of employment, put out the dumpster fires known as Burnetts and empower the cubicle camaraderies known as Burnetts!

DR. TRACEY C. JONES
AUTHOR, SPEAKER, GREATNESS IGNITOR

Dr. Tracey C. Jones is a results-generating operations professional with extensive experience directing production teams, technical personnel, and line management staffs in exceeding production goals and objectives. Her key strengths involve Strategic Vision, Mission Planning, Complex Problem Solving, and Technical Program Management. She served twelve years as a Commissioned Officer in the United States Air Force with expertise as a logistician and fighter aircraft maintenance officer. She received numerous medals and commendations for her deployment during the first Gulf War (Operation DESERT SHIELD/DESERT STORM), as well as the Bosnian War. She also participated in numerous UN peacekeeping deployments to Incirlik AB, Turkey as part of Operation Northern Watch.

Upon exiting the military, Ms. Jones spent the next five years in a Fortune 500 Semiconductor Company directing pilot and volume manufacturing lines. She then stepped into Engineering Program Expertise in a defense contracting company designing new technologies for the war fighter in the Space Technology division. Ms. Jones then demonstrated her operational expertise directing a large, diverse Base Operations Service Contract (BOSC) for the National Geospatial Intelligence Agency

(NGA) located in Saint Louis, MO, where she retained the highest governmental clearances.

When her father, the legendary Charlie "Tremendous" Jones, passed away in 2008, Dr. Jones took the reigns of his company, Executive Books, and transformed it into one of the country's top publishing and leadership content providers.

Dr. Jones' education credentials include an AA from the New Mexico Military Institute, a BS from the United States Air Force Academy, an MBA in Global Management, and a PhD in Leadership from Lancaster Bible College.

She is an in-demand leadership expert known for her expertise as well as her ability to connect on a core level with her audiences as she masterfully weaves leadership concepts and actionable strategies together with humor and a deep understanding of life in the workplace. Her company, Tremendous Leadership, has donated $1.6M over the past ten years to homeless shelters, disaster relief organizations, scholarships to local colleges, and animal rescues. She is the author of ten leadership books and runs a robust publishing house. Dr. Jones also hosts the weekly Leaders on Leadership podcast.

Dr. Jones was awarded the TFEC Women in Philanthropy Award; Leadership Cumberland Award and West Shore Chamber of Commerce Business of the Year Award. In 2017, she received an honorary doctorate from Central Penn College, one of two local institutions of higher learning that house libraries honoring her father's legacy. As a self-proclaimed "bibliotherapist," Dr. Jones conducts character development and reading programs in elementary schools and homeless shelters, as well as several Pennsylvania state penitentiaries. She serves as a board member for Bethesda Mission in Harrisburg, PA, as well as the Penn Mutual Center for Veteran's Affairs. She is passionate about the power of divine transformation through mind renewal. When she's not researching or writing, Dr. Jones can be found adding rescue dogs and cats to her ever-expanding "fur family."

BOOKS

Dr. Jones has written eleven books. Here is a curated collection of the essential Dr. Jones.

SPARK*: 5 Essentials to Ignite the Greatness Within*
A Message to Millennials*: What Your Employee Needs You to Know and Your Parents Didn't Tell You*
Beyond Tremendous*: Raising the Bar on Life*
True Blue Leadership: *Top Ten Ways to Lead Your Pack*
Saucy Aussie Living*: Top Ten Ways to Get a Second Leash on Life*

KEYNOTES

Bring Dr. Jones in for a keynote you'll never forget! Topics include:

Take This Job and Love It • There's No Such Thing as Leadership…Without Followership • Unleashing the Leader Within • The Science of Success • Building the Dream Team • Cultivating Emerging Leaders • The Mystery of Self-Motivation • The Price of Leadership

CORPORATE WORKSHOPS

Dr. Jones is known for her targeted, transformative, and tremendous Corporate Workshops. Why? Because they work. Topics include:

The Seven Laws of Leadership • The Seven Functions of Followership • Confident Decision-Making • Breakthrough to Excellence • Critical Thinking Skills • Ethical-Decision Making • Teams and Trust • Crisis Leadership and Resilient Teams

STRATEGIC PLANNING

Bring Dr. Jones into your organization to gather input for your strategic plans. Clarify your vision. Get the boost you need to achieve the heights you desire—and deserve.

MERGERS & ACQUISITIONS

Is your organization proposing or going through a merger or acquisition? Has it already completed one? Dr. Jones has extensive experience researching organizations contemplating or executing a merger or acquisition. Merging organizations is easy; merging people is hard. Everyone processes change differently. What is business as usual to one team member may be the end of the world to another. When you deal with mergers/acquisitions you've got one side that has the upper hand while the other feels more vulnerable. Never underestimate how quickly your preferred future can be interpreted as the beginning of the end.

EXECUTIVE MENTORING

Leadership is both art and science. You'll need someone by your side to guide you through the unexpected, the politics, and the obstacles. Dr. Jones has risen to the top tier in four different industries. She knows what it takes to claim your seat at the table and ensure you've got the full support of your chain of command and team members. Reach out for one-on-one executive-level mentoring so you can gain those best insights into your current phase of life or career level. Reach out to Dr. Jones today at ***www.TraceyCJones.com***.

**CONNECT WITH
DR. TRACEY C. JONES**

TraceyCJones.com

TremendousLeadership.com

in *drtraceycjones*

f *TremendousTracey*

t *TraceyCJones*